I0490767

NATURAL RESOURCES LAW: MANAGING CONFLICTS BETWEEN RESOURCE EXTRACTION AND CONSERVATION

Muhammad Khalid Aziz Bari

Copyright © 2023 Muhammad Khalid Aziz Bari

All rights reserved

No part of this book may be reproduced, or stored in a retrieval system,
or transmitted in any form or by any means, electronic, mechanical,
photocopying, recording, or otherwise, without express written permission
of the publisher.

ISBN: 9798388828224

Cover design by: Art Painter
Printed in the United States of America

This book is dedicated to all those who are working to preserve our planet's natural resources for future generations. It is also dedicated to those who have been affected by conflicts between resource extraction and conservation, and to those who strive to find solutions to these complex issues.

"The earth has music for those who listen."

GEORGE SANTAYANA

CONTENTS

INTRODUCTION

Natural resources are essential to our daily lives, providing the raw materials and energy necessary to support our modern way of life. However, the extraction and use of natural resources can also have negative impacts on the environment, including habitat destruction, water pollution, and climate change. Balancing the interests of resource extraction and conservation is a complex and challenging task, one that is at the heart of natural resources law.

The field of natural resources law encompasses a wide range of legal frameworks and regulations that govern the use, management, and protection of natural resources. From international treaties to national laws and regulations, natural resources law plays a critical role in ensuring the sustainable use of our planet's resources.

In recent years, conflicts between resource extraction and conservation have become increasingly common, as growing demand for natural resources has put pressure on ecosystems and biodiversity. These conflicts can arise between governments and communities, between resource extraction companies and conservation organizations, and even between different sectors of the resource extraction industry itself.

This book, "Natural Resources Law: Managing Conflicts Between Resource Extraction and Conservation," provides a comprehensive overview of the legal framework for natural resources law and explores the conflicts that arise between resource extraction and conservation. Through case studies and analysis, we examine the complex balancing act that is required to ensure that natural resources are managed in a sustainable and responsible way.

In the following chapters, we will explore the different types of natural resources, the legal framework for natural resources law, and the tools and techniques that are used to manage conflicts between resource extraction and conservation. We will also examine case studies from around the world that illustrate the challenges and opportunities of natural resources law.

As the world faces increasing environmental challenges, the role of natural resources law has become more critical than ever. By providing a framework for the sustainable use of natural resources, natural resources law can help to ensure that future generations have access to the resources they need to thrive.

We will also explore the future directions of natural resources law, including the role of technology in resource extraction and conservation, the impacts of climate change on natural resources, and the need for sustainable and ecosystem-based management practices.

As we delve into the complexities of natural resources law, it is important to remember that there are no easy solutions to the conflicts that arise between resource extraction and conservation. Balancing the competing interests of industry, government, and environmental groups requires careful consideration of social, economic, and environmental factors.

However, through collaboration and innovation, it is possible to find solutions that can benefit all stakeholders, including the environment, local communities, and the economy. By exploring the challenges and opportunities of natural resources law, we hope to inspire a deeper understanding of the complex issues that surround the management of our planet's resources.

Ultimately, the goal of this book is to provide a comprehensive overview of natural resources law and to stimulate discussion and debate on the complex issues that surround the sustainable use of natural resources. We hope that this book will serve as a valuable resource for policymakers, legal practitioners, environmental groups, and anyone interested in the management of our planet's natural resources.

We believe that a deeper understanding of the legal framework and management practices of natural resources can lead to more informed decision-making and ultimately, a more sustainable future. The challenges facing natural resources management are significant, but we remain hopeful that through cooperation and dialogue, we can find solutions that balance the needs of society with the protection of our planet's natural resources.

We encourage readers to engage with the material presented in this book, to critically evaluate the case studies and legal frameworks presented, and to consider their own role in shaping the future of natural resources law. By working together, we can create a more sustainable and equitable future for all.

In the following chapters, we will explore the complexities of natural resources law and management, beginning with an overview of the legal framework and the challenges of balancing resource extraction and conservation. We will then examine the different types of natural resources, the management tools and techniques used to resolve conflicts, and case studies from around the world that illustrate the challenges and opportunities of natural resources law.

We hope that this book will serve as a useful resource for anyone interested in the sustainable use of natural resources, and we look forward to exploring this critical issue with you.

As we embark on this journey, it is important to acknowledge that natural resources law is a rapidly evolving field, shaped by technological advancements, changing societal values, and the urgent need to address global environmental challenges. It is our hope that this book will contribute to the ongoing dialogue and research on the complex issues surrounding natural resources law.

Furthermore, we recognize that natural resources are often at the center of complex social, economic, and political dynamics that involve diverse stakeholders with competing interests. Our aim is to present a balanced perspective on the challenges of managing conflicts between resource extraction and conservation, while recognizing the diverse perspectives and values of different stakeholders.

Finally, we wish to express our gratitude to the many experts, scholars, and practitioners who have contributed to the development of natural resources law and management. It is through their efforts that we have gained a deeper understanding of the complexities of this field and the importance of sustainable resource management.

We hope that this book will contribute to the ongoing dialogue and research on natural resources law and inspire further collaboration and innovation in the field. We invite you to join us on this journey as we explore the challenges and opportunities of managing conflicts between resource extraction and conservation.

PREFACE

Natural resource management is one of the most complex and pressing challenges of our time. As human populations continue to grow, the demand for resources increases, and conflicts between resource extraction and conservation become more frequent and complex. The legal framework for natural resource management is diverse and constantly evolving, and it is essential to understand this framework to effectively manage our planet's resources.

This book, "Natural Resources Law: Managing Conflicts Between Resource Extraction and Conservation," provides a comprehensive overview of the legal framework for natural resource management and the challenges that arise in balancing resource extraction with conservation. We draw on our extensive experience in the field to offer insights from legal, policy, and scientific perspectives. We also provide case studies from around the world to illustrate the complexities of natural resource management and the diverse strategies used to address conflicts.

We wrote this book to provide a valuable resource for students, scholars, practitioners, and policymakers working in the field of natural resources law and management. Our hope is that this book will help readers understand the complex legal framework for natural resource management, the challenges that arise in balancing resource extraction with conservation, and the diverse strategies used to address conflicts. We also hope that this book will inspire and inform those who are working to find solutions to these critical issues.

We would like to express our gratitude to all those who have contributed to this book, including our colleagues, friends, and families. We also thank our publisher for their support and guidance throughout the process.

PROLOGUE

The management of natural resources is one of the greatest challenges facing our planet. Human populations are growing, and the demand for resources continues to increase. This demand puts pressure on our planet's ecosystems, threatening biodiversity, and undermining the ability of ecosystems to provide the essential services that we rely on.

Managing natural resources is a complex and multi-faceted challenge, and there are no easy solutions. Resource extraction can generate significant economic benefits, but it can also have negative impacts on the environment and the communities that depend on these resources. Conservation, on the other hand, is essential for maintaining the health and functioning of ecosystems, but it can also limit access to resources and generate conflicts between different stakeholders.

In this book, we explore the legal framework for managing natural resources, and we examine the challenges that arise in balancing resource extraction with conservation. We draw on case studies from around the world to illustrate the complexities of natural resource management and the diverse strategies used to address conflicts.

Our hope is that this book will provide a valuable resource for students, scholars, practitioners, and policymakers working in the field of natural resources law and management. We also hope that this book will inspire and inform those who are working to find solutions to the complex challenges facing our planet's ecosystems.

As we embark on this journey, we invite you to join us in exploring the fascinating and complex world of natural resources law and management.

CHAPTER 1: INTRODUCTION TO NATURAL RESOURCES LAW

Natural resources are materials and substances that occur naturally in the environment and are used by humans for economic and social purposes. These resources include minerals, water, land, forests, and energy sources such as oil, natural gas, and renewable energy. Natural resources are essential to the functioning of modern societies and are used in everything from food production to construction, transportation, and manufacturing.

The extraction and use of natural resources can have both positive and negative impacts on the environment. Resource extraction can lead to habitat destruction, water pollution, and climate change. On the other hand, the conservation of natural resources is essential for maintaining ecosystem health, preserving biodiversity, and supporting the well-being of communities that rely on these resources.

The legal framework for natural resources law is designed to address these competing interests by providing a set of rules and regulations that govern the use, management, and protection of natural resources. These rules and regulations are established at both the international and national levels and are enforced by governments, courts, and other regulatory bodies.

At the international level, natural resources law is governed by a variety of treaties and agreements, such as the United Nations Convention on the Law of the Sea, which sets out the legal framework for the use and management of ocean resources. Other international agreements, such as the Convention on Biological Diversity and the Paris Agreement on climate change, provide a framework for protecting natural resources and promoting sustainability.

At the national level, natural resources law is established through a variety of legal frameworks, including constitutional law, property law, and environmental law. These laws and regulations establish the rights and responsibilities of governments, individuals, and companies in the use and management of natural resources.

Environmental impact assessment is one of the most important tools in natural resources law. Environmental impact assessment is a process that identifies and evaluates the potential environmental impacts of a proposed project or activity. This process helps to ensure that resource extraction activities are conducted in a sustainable and responsible manner, with appropriate measures taken to mitigate any negative impacts.

Natural resources law is a constantly evolving field that responds to changing social, economic, and environmental conditions. As the world faces increasing environmental challenges, such as climate change, natural resources law has become more critical than ever. The legal framework for natural resources law must adapt to these changing conditions in order to ensure the long-term sustainability of natural resources.

One of the key challenges of natural resources law is managing conflicts between resource extraction and conservation. These conflicts can arise between governments and communities, between resource extraction companies and conservation organizations, and even between different sectors of the resource extraction industry itself. Conflicts can arise over issues such as land use, water management, pollution, and biodiversity conservation.

One approach to managing conflicts between resource extraction and conservation is to use a collaborative or participatory approach. This approach involves engaging all stakeholders in the decision-making process and ensuring that their voices are heard. By bringing together different perspectives and interests, a collaborative approach can lead to more sustainable and equitable outcomes.

Another approach to managing conflicts is through the use of market-based instruments, such as taxes, fees, and tradable permits. These instruments can provide incentives for companies to reduce their environmental impact and can also generate revenue that can be used for conservation efforts.

Natural resources law also plays an important role in promoting social justice and human rights. Many communities around the world rely on natural resources for their livelihoods and cultural identity. Ensuring that these communities are involved in decisions about the use and management of natural resources is essential for protecting their rights and promoting social justice.

In addition, natural resources law can help to promote sustainable development, which seeks to meet the needs of the present without compromising the ability of future generations to meet their own needs. By promoting sustainable resource use and management, natural resources law can help to ensure that future generations have access to the resources they need to thrive.

As the world population continues to grow and demand for natural resources increases, managing conflicts between resource extraction and conservation will become more important than ever. Climate change and environmental degradation are already having a significant impact on natural resources and the communities that rely on them. It is therefore essential that natural resources law continues to evolve and adapt in order to address these challenges.

One of the key trends in natural resources law is the shift towards a more integrated and holistic approach. This approach recognizes that natural resources are interconnected and that decisions about resource use and management must consider their social, economic, and environmental impacts.

This integrated approach requires collaboration between different sectors and stakeholders, as well as a commitment to transparency and accountability.

Another trend in natural resources law is the increasing recognition of the rights of indigenous peoples and local communities. These communities have often been marginalized and excluded from decision-making processes around natural resources. However, there is growing recognition that they have a unique knowledge and perspective that is essential for sustainable resource use and management. Ensuring that these communities are involved in decisions about natural resources is not only a matter of social justice, but also essential for promoting sustainable development.

Technology is also playing an increasingly important role in natural resources law. New technologies, such as remote sensing and artificial intelligence, are providing new tools for monitoring and managing natural resources. However, there are also concerns about the impact of new technologies on natural resources and the communities that rely on them. It is therefore essential that natural resources law keep pace with these technological developments in order to ensure that they are used in a responsible and sustainable manner.

Chapter 1 also provides an overview of the major natural resources that are subject to legal regulation. These include minerals, oil and gas, forests, water, fisheries, and biodiversity. Each of these resources presents unique challenges in terms of managing conflicts between resource extraction and conservation.

For example, the extraction of minerals can have significant environmental impacts, such as water pollution and soil degradation. At the same time, minerals are essential for modern society, and demand for them is only expected to increase. Natural resources law must therefore balance the need for resource extraction with the need to protect the environment and the rights of communities that may be affected by mining activities.

Similarly, oil and gas extraction can have significant

environmental impacts, including greenhouse gas emissions that contribute to climate change. However, oil and gas are critical for meeting global energy demand. Natural resources law must therefore promote the development of alternative energy sources while also ensuring that oil and gas extraction is conducted in a responsible and sustainable manner.

Forests are another critical natural resource that is subject to legal regulation. Forests provide important ecosystem services, such as carbon sequestration and biodiversity conservation. At the same time, forests are often subject to deforestation and degradation due to commercial logging and other human activities. Natural resources law must therefore balance the need for economic development with the need to protect forests and the communities that rely on them.

Water is another essential natural resource that is subject to legal regulation. Water scarcity is becoming an increasingly pressing issue in many parts of the world, and conflicts over water use and management are becoming more common. Natural resources law must therefore ensure that water resources are managed in a sustainable and equitable manner.

Fisheries are another critical natural resource that is subject to legal regulation. Overfishing and other unsustainable practices have led to declining fish populations and marine biodiversity. Natural resources law must therefore promote sustainable fisheries management in order to ensure that fish stocks are replenished and the livelihoods of fishing communities are protected.

Finally, biodiversity is a critical natural resource that is subject to legal regulation. Biodiversity loss is one of the most pressing environmental challenges facing the world today, and natural resources law must play a key role in protecting biodiversity and promoting its conservation.

In summary, Chapter 1 provides an overview of the key concepts and trends in natural resources law, as well as an introduction to the major natural resources that are subject to legal regulation. By understanding these concepts and trends, readers will be better equipped to understand the complex and multifaceted issues that arise in managing conflicts between resource extraction and conservation.

CHAPTER 2: THE LEGAL FRAMEWORK FOR NATURAL RESOURCES LAW

Natural resources law is a complex and multifaceted field that is governed by a wide range of international and national laws and regulations. These laws and regulations provide the legal framework for managing conflicts between resource extraction and conservation. Chapter 2 provides an overview of the major international and national legal instruments that govern natural resources law.

International Legal Framework

The United Nations (UN) and its specialized agencies play a key role in developing and implementing international legal instruments that govern natural resources law. Some of the most important UN instruments include:

1.   The United Nations Framework Convention on Climate Change (UNFCCC): This is a treaty that was adopted in 1992 with the goal of stabilizing greenhouse gas concentrations in the atmosphere at a level that would prevent dangerous anthropogenic interference with the climate system. The UNFCCC has been ratified by 197 parties, making it one of the most widely ratified international environmental treaties.

2.   The Convention on Biological Diversity (CBD): This is a

treaty that was adopted in 1992 with the goal of promoting the conservation and sustainable use of biodiversity. The CBD has been ratified by 196 parties and is considered one of the most important international environmental agreements.

3.   The United Nations Convention on the Law of the Sea (UNCLOS): This is a treaty that was adopted in 1982 with the goal of providing a comprehensive legal framework for the management of the world's oceans and their resources. UNCLOS has been ratified by 168 parties and is widely regarded as one of the most important international legal instruments for managing natural resources.

National Legal Framework

In addition to international legal instruments, natural resources law is also governed by national laws and regulations. These laws and regulations vary from country to country, but they generally provide the legal framework for managing natural resources within a particular jurisdiction. Some of the most important national legal instruments include:

1.   Mining Laws: Mining laws govern the exploration, development, and extraction of minerals. These laws vary from country to country, but they generally provide for the granting of mineral rights, the regulation of mining activities, and the payment of royalties and other fees.

2.   Water Laws: Water laws govern the management and allocation of water resources. These laws vary from country to country, but they generally provide for the allocation of water rights, the regulation of water use, and the protection of water quality.

3.   Fisheries Laws: Fisheries laws govern the management and conservation of fish populations. These laws vary from country to country, but they generally provide for the regulation of fishing activities, the protection of marine ecosystems, and the allocation of fishing rights.

4.   Forest Laws: Forest laws govern the management and

conservation of forest resources. These laws vary from country to country, but they generally provide for the regulation of logging activities, the protection of forest ecosystems, and the allocation of forest rights.

Moreover, the legal framework for natural resources law is constantly evolving as new environmental challenges arise and new technologies are developed for resource extraction and conservation. For example, the rise of renewable energy technologies has led to the development of new legal instruments and policies aimed at promoting the use of clean energy sources and reducing greenhouse gas emissions. Similarly, advances in biotechnology and genetic engineering have raised new challenges for the conservation and sustainable use of biodiversity, leading to the development of new legal frameworks and regulations.

In addition to the legal framework, natural resources law is also shaped by other factors such as social, economic, and cultural considerations. For example, the distribution of natural resources can have significant impacts on the economic development and social well-being of local communities. The rights of indigenous peoples and local communities to participate in decision-making processes related to natural resource management are also important considerations in natural resources law.

Finally, natural resources law is often characterized by conflicts between different stakeholders with competing interests. These conflicts can arise between government agencies, private companies, local communities, environmental organizations, and other stakeholders. Effective management of these conflicts requires a deep understanding of the legal framework and other factors shaping natural resources law, as well as strong communication and negotiation skills.

As the world's population continues to grow and global demand for natural resources increases, the need for effective natural resources management becomes more urgent than ever. The legal framework for natural resources law provides an essential tool for achieving sustainable management of these resources, balancing the needs of economic development with the imperative to protect the environment and conserve biodiversity.

In the following chapters of this book, we will delve deeper into the specific legal issues and challenges facing different sectors of natural resources law, such as mining, water management, fisheries, and forests. We will explore the ways in which international and national legal instruments are applied in practice, and examine case studies from different parts of the world to illustrate the complex and diverse issues that arise in natural resources management.

In the upcoming chapters, we will discuss the various legal instruments and frameworks that govern natural resources law, including international conventions and treaties, regional agreements, and national laws and regulations. We will also explore the role of institutions and organizations involved in natural resources management, including government agencies, non-governmental organizations, and community-based organizations.

Chapter 3 will focus specifically on the legal framework for mining and extractive industries, which has been a particularly contentious area in natural resources law. We will discuss the international and national laws and regulations that govern mining activities, including environmental and social impact assessments, community consultation and participation, and compensation for affected communities. We will also examine the challenges associated with enforcing these laws and ensuring compliance by mining companies.

Chapter 4 will delve into the legal framework for water management, which is becoming an increasingly pressing issue in many parts of the world as demand for water resources grows and water scarcity becomes more prevalent. We will discuss the different legal frameworks for water management, including water rights and allocation systems, and examine case studies of successful water management initiatives.

Chapter 5 will focus on the legal framework for fisheries

management, which is a complex and multifaceted area of natural resources law. We will discuss the international and national laws and regulations that govern fisheries management, including regulations for fishing quotas and fishing gear, and examine the challenges associated with ensuring sustainable fisheries management in a globalized economy.

Finally, in Chapter 6, we will examine the legal framework for forest management, which is critical for the conservation of biodiversity and the mitigation of climate change. We will discuss the different legal instruments and frameworks for forest management, including international conventions and national laws, and examine the challenges associated with implementing these laws and ensuring sustainable forest management.

By the end of this book, readers will have a thorough understanding of the legal framework for natural resources law and the complex issues and challenges facing the sustainable management of our planet's natural resources. We hope that this book will inspire readers to become more engaged in the global effort to protect our natural resources and promote sustainable development.

CHAPTER 3: TYPES OF NATURAL RESOURCES

Natural resources are the materials and substances that occur naturally on Earth and are used by humans for various purposes. They are vital for human survival and economic development, but they are also finite and vulnerable to overuse and exploitation. In this chapter, we will discuss the different types of natural resources and the legal framework for their management.

1.Mineral Resources

Mineral resources are the naturally occurring substances found in the earth's crust that have economic value. They include metallic minerals such as gold, copper, and iron, as well as non-metallic minerals such as salt, coal, and oil. The extraction and use of mineral resources are critical for economic development, but they also have significant environmental and social impacts, including habitat destruction, water pollution, and displacement of local communities.

The legal framework for mineral resources management varies widely depending on the country and the type of mineral being extracted. In some countries, mining is governed by a comprehensive set of laws and regulations that address environmental and social concerns, while in other countries, the legal framework is less developed, and mining activities may occur with little oversight or regulation.

2.Water Resources

Water resources are the natural sources of freshwater, including rivers, lakes, and groundwater, that are essential for human survival and economic development. They are also critical for maintaining healthy ecosystems and supporting biodiversity. The management of water resources involves balancing competing demands for water, such as agricultural irrigation, domestic use, and industrial needs, with the imperative to protect the environment and conserve water resources for future generations.

The legal framework for water resources management includes laws and regulations that govern water allocation, water quality, and water use. These laws vary widely depending on the country and the specific water resource in question. In some countries, water rights are tradable, allowing users to buy and sell water allocations, while in other countries, water resources are owned by the state, and access is regulated through permits and licenses.

3.Fisheries Resources

Fisheries resources are the fish and other aquatic animals and plants that are harvested for food and other purposes. They are critical for human nutrition and livelihoods, but they are also vulnerable to overfishing and habitat destruction. The management of fisheries resources involves balancing the economic benefits of fishing with the need to protect fish populations and their ecosystems.

The legal framework for fisheries management includes regulations for fishing quotas, fishing gear, and fishing methods, as well as rules for monitoring and enforcing these regulations. These laws vary widely depending on the country and the type of fishery in question. In some countries, fishing is governed by a comprehensive set of laws and regulations that aim to ensure sustainable fisheries management, while in other countries, the legal framework may be less developed, and overfishing and illegal fishing may occur with little oversight or regulation.

4.Forest Resources

Forest resources are the trees and other vegetation that cover the earth's surface and provide a wide range of ecosystem services, including carbon sequestration, soil conservation, and biodiversity conservation. They are also critical for human needs such as timber, fuelwood, and non-timber forest products. The management of forest resources involves balancing the economic benefits of forest exploitation with the need to protect forest ecosystems and biodiversity.

The legal framework for forest management includes laws and regulations that govern forest ownership, access, and use, as well as rules for forest conservation and reforestation. These laws vary widely depending on the country and the type of forest in question. In some countries, forest management is governed by a comprehensive set of laws and regulations that aim to ensure sustainable forest management, while in other countries, the legal framework may be less developed, and forest destruction may occur with little oversight or regulation.

Effective management of natural resources requires a deep understanding of the legal framework and the different types of natural resources. In this chapter, we have discussed four types of natural resources: mineral resources, water resources, fisheries resources, and forest resources. We have also examined the legal framework for managing these resources and the challenges associated with their exploitation and conservation.

In the next chapter, we will focus on the conflicts that often arise between resource extraction and conservation, and the legal and policy tools available to manage these conflicts. We will explore the concept of sustainable development and its application in the context of natural resources management. We will also discuss the role of stakeholders, including local communities, in the management of natural resources and the importance of their participation in decision-making processes.

Furthermore, this chapter also highlighted the importance of adopting a holistic approach to natural resource management, which takes into account not only the economic benefits but also the social and environmental costs associated with their extraction and utilization. The legal framework for managing natural resources must balance the interests of different stakeholders, including governments, private companies, local communities, and environmental organizations.

The extraction of natural resources can have significant economic benefits, but it can also have negative impacts on the environment and local communities. For example, mining activities can lead to soil erosion, water pollution, and destruction of habitats. Fishing practices that are not sustainable can lead to the depletion of fish stocks and the loss of livelihoods for fishing communities. Similarly, the uncontrolled exploitation of forests can lead to deforestation, soil degradation, and loss of biodiversity.

The legal framework for managing natural resources must, therefore, be designed to ensure that resource extraction is carried out in a manner that is socially and environmentally responsible. This requires the development of policies and regulations that promote sustainable resource use and conservation.

In the next chapter, we will explore the conflicts that often arise between resource extraction and conservation, and the legal and policy tools available to manage these conflicts. We will also discuss the importance of sustainable development in the management of natural resources and the role of stakeholders in decision-making processes.

Moreover, the legal framework for natural resource management must also take into account the need to address the social and economic impacts of resource extraction on local communities. For instance, mining activities can lead to the displacement of communities and the loss of traditional livelihoods. Similarly, the depletion of fish stocks can have significant impacts on the livelihoods of fishing communities.

To address these challenges, the legal framework must ensure that the interests of local communities are taken into account in decision-making processes. This can be achieved through the implementation of policies and regulations that promote the participation of local communities in natural resource management. It is also important to ensure that local communities are adequately compensated for any adverse impacts on their livelihoods.

Chapter 3 has emphasized that natural resources are not unlimited, and their exploitation must be balanced with conservation efforts to ensure their sustainability for future generations. This requires a legal framework that promotes sustainable development and considers the interests of different stakeholders. It is essential to recognize that the management of natural resources is not solely a legal issue but also a social, economic, and environmental one.

In the next chapter, we will explore the conflicts that often arise between resource extraction and conservation and the legal and policy tools available to manage these conflicts. We will examine the concept of sustainable development and how it can guide natural resource management decisions. We will also discuss the role of stakeholders in decision-making processes and the importance of their participation in natural resource management.

Furthermore, the chapter will examine the challenges associated with implementing sustainable natural resource management policies and the different approaches that can be used to address these challenges. We will also explore the role of international law in natural resource management and its impact on national laws and policies.

In conclusion, the legal framework for natural resource management must strike a balance between resource extraction and conservation, taking into account the interests of different stakeholders. The next chapter will provide an in-depth analysis of the conflicts that arise between resource extraction and conservation and the legal and policy tools available to manage these conflicts.

CHAPTER 4: MANAGING CONFLICTS BETWEEN RESOURCE EXTRACTION AND CONSERVATION

Natural resources are essential for economic development and human well-being, but their extraction can have negative impacts on the environment and local communities. Conflicts often arise between resource extraction and conservation, and managing these conflicts requires a comprehensive legal and policy framework.

This chapter will explore the conflicts that arise between resource extraction and conservation and the legal and policy tools available to manage these conflicts. It will examine the concept of sustainable development and how it can guide natural resource management decisions. The chapter will also discuss the role of stakeholders in decision-making processes and the importance of their participation in natural resource management.

Sustainable Development

Sustainable development is a guiding principle for natural resource management that seeks to meet the needs of the present without compromising the ability of future generations to meet their own needs. It recognizes that economic development, social well-being, and environmental protection are interdependent and must be integrated in decision-making processes.

The concept of sustainable development has been enshrined in international law through the adoption of the Sustainable Development Goals (SDGs) by the United Nations General Assembly. The SDGs provide a framework for sustainable development that addresses a range of issues, including poverty, inequality, climate change, and natural resource management.

Stakeholder Participation

Stakeholder participation is essential for effective natural resource management. It ensures that the interests of different stakeholders are taken into account in decision-making processes and promotes transparency and accountability. Stakeholders can include governments, private companies, local communities, and environmental organizations.

Stakeholder participation can take many forms, including public consultations, community meetings, and stakeholder engagement processes. It is important to ensure that stakeholders have access to relevant information and resources to enable meaningful participation.

Legal and Policy Tools

There are several legal and policy tools available to manage conflicts between resource extraction and conservation. These include:

1. Environmental Impact Assessment (EIA): EIAs are a tool for identifying and assessing the potential environmental impacts of proposed projects. They are used to inform decision-making processes and ensure that the environmental impacts of projects are taken into account.

2. Strategic Environmental Assessment (SEA): SEAs are a tool for assessing the potential environmental impacts of

policies, plans, and programs. They are used to ensure that the environmental impacts of these instruments are taken into account in decision-making processes.

3.   Environmental Regulations: Environmental regulations are legal instruments that set standards and requirements for resource extraction activities. They are used to ensure that resource extraction activities are carried out in a manner that is socially and environmentally responsible.

4.   Conservation Measures: Conservation measures are policies and practices that aim to protect and conserve natural resources. They can include protected areas, wildlife corridors, and sustainable use policies.

In addition to the legal and policy tools discussed above, it is also important to consider the role of ethical considerations in managing conflicts between resource extraction and conservation. Ethical considerations can include the rights of indigenous peoples and local communities, the protection of cultural heritage sites, and the prevention of environmental harm.

Indigenous peoples and local communities often have a close relationship with natural resources and can be disproportionately affected by resource extraction activities. It is important to recognize and respect their rights and involve them in decision-making processes.

Cultural heritage sites, such as sacred sites, can also be impacted by resource extraction activities. It is important to take measures to protect these sites and ensure that they are not irreparably damaged or destroyed.

Finally, preventing environmental harm should be a key consideration in managing conflicts between resource extraction and conservation. This can include minimizing the use of hazardous substances, reducing greenhouse gas emissions, and avoiding the destruction of sensitive ecosystems.

To effectively manage conflicts between resource extraction and conservation, it is important to consider all of these factors and balance them appropriately. This can be a challenging task, as different stakeholders may have competing interests and priorities.

One approach to managing conflicts is through the use of stakeholder engagement and consultation processes. This can involve engaging with affected communities and other stakeholders to understand their perspectives and concerns, and incorporating this feedback into decision-making processes.

Another approach is to use impact assessments to evaluate the potential environmental, social, and economic impacts of resource extraction activities. These assessments can help to identify potential risks and opportunities and inform decision-making.

Regulatory frameworks and enforcement mechanisms can also play a key role in managing conflicts between resource extraction and conservation. Governments can use laws and regulations to set standards and requirements for resource extraction activities and to ensure that companies comply with these requirements.

Finally, effective monitoring and reporting mechanisms are essential to ensuring that resource extraction activities are managed in a way that promotes conservation and environmental protection. This can involve regular monitoring of environmental indicators, as well as reporting and transparency mechanisms that enable stakeholders to hold companies and governments accountable for their actions.

It is important to note that managing conflicts between resource extraction and conservation is not a one-time event but rather an ongoing process that requires regular review and adaptation. As new technologies and practices emerge, it may be necessary to update legal frameworks and regulatory requirements to ensure that they remain relevant and effective.

Moreover, the management of natural resources requires a long-term perspective. This means that decisions made today will have implications for future generations. Therefore, it is essential to consider the long-term impacts of resource extraction activities and to take steps to ensure that natural resources are managed in a sustainable and responsible manner.

In conclusion, the effective management of conflicts between resource extraction and conservation is crucial to ensuring sustainable development and the protection of natural resources. By adopting a comprehensive approach that takes into account legal and policy frameworks, stakeholder engagement, ethical considerations, impact assessments, regulatory frameworks, and monitoring and reporting mechanisms, we can ensure that natural resources are managed in a way that promotes economic development, social well-being, and environmental protection for present and future generations.

CHAPTER 5: CASE STUDIES IN NATURAL RESOURCES LAW

In this chapter, we will examine several case studies that highlight the challenges and opportunities associated with managing conflicts between resource extraction and conservation. These case studies represent a diverse range of natural resources, geographic locations, and stakeholders, and provide insights into the complex legal, social, and environmental issues that arise when natural resources are extracted.

1.The Bakken Oil Fields

The Bakken Oil Fields, located in North Dakota and Montana, are a major source of crude oil in the United States. The development of these oil fields has led to significant economic growth in the region, but has also raised concerns about the environmental and social impacts of oil extraction.

One of the key challenges in managing conflicts in the Bakken Oil Fields has been balancing the economic benefits of oil extraction with the need to protect the environment and public health. The oil fields have been associated with a range of environmental impacts, including air and water pollution, habitat destruction, and the release of greenhouse gases.

To address these concerns, the US government has implemented a range of regulatory measures, including air and water quality standards, waste management requirements, and restrictions on drilling in certain areas. However, there is ongoing debate about the effectiveness of these measures and whether they go far enough to protect the environment and public health.

2.The Kimberley Process Certification Scheme

The Kimberley Process Certification Scheme is an international agreement aimed at preventing the trade of conflict diamonds, which are diamonds that are mined in areas of conflict and sold to finance armed conflict against governments. The scheme requires participating countries to certify that their diamond exports are conflict-free and to put in place measures to prevent the trade of conflict diamonds.

The Kimberley Process Certification Scheme represents a successful example of using legal and regulatory frameworks to manage conflicts associated with natural resource extraction. The scheme has helped to reduce the trade in conflict diamonds and has provided a mechanism for countries to work together to prevent the financing of armed conflict.

However, the scheme has also been criticized for not going far enough to address other social and environmental concerns associated with diamond mining, such as labor rights abuses, environmental degradation, and the displacement of local communities.

3.The Palm Oil Industry in Indonesia

The palm oil industry in Indonesia represents another example of the challenges associated with managing conflicts between resource extraction and conservation. The industry has been associated with deforestation, habitat destruction, and the displacement of indigenous communities.

To address these concerns, the Indonesian government has implemented a range of legal and regulatory measures, including restrictions on land use, certification schemes for sustainable palm oil production, and penalties for illegal logging and land clearing.

However, there is ongoing debate about the effectiveness of these measures and the extent to which they are being enforced. Moreover, there are concerns that the palm oil industry may be contributing to climate change by releasing large amounts of greenhouse gases through deforestation and peatland degradation.

4.Mining in the Democratic Republic of Congo

Mining in the Democratic Republic of Congo (DRC) is another example of the complex legal and social issues associated with natural resource extraction. The DRC is rich in minerals such as cobalt, copper, and gold, which are used in a range of consumer products, including smartphones and electric vehicles.

However, the mining industry in the DRC has been associated with a range of social and environmental concerns, including child labor, human rights abuses, and environmental degradation. Moreover, the profits from mining activities have often been used to fund armed conflict and corruption.

To address these concerns, the DRC government has implemented a range of legal and regulatory measures, including restrictions on child labor, penalties for human rights abuses, and environmental protection requirements. However, the implementation and enforcement of these measures has been challenging, and there are ongoing concerns about the effectiveness of these measures in protecting human rights and the environment.

In this chapter, we will explore several case studies that highlight the complex legal and practical issues that arise when balancing resource extraction and conservation. Each case study illustrates the challenges that policymakers, industry leaders, and environmentalists face when navigating natural resource management.

1.   The Arctic National Wildlife Refuge: The debate over oil drilling in the Arctic National Wildlife Refuge (ANWR) has been ongoing for decades. Proponents argue that drilling would create

jobs, increase domestic oil production, and boost the economy. Opponents, on the other hand, point out that the ANWR is home to many species of wildlife, including caribou and polar bears, and that drilling would cause significant environmental harm. The legal battle over whether to allow drilling in the ANWR has been fought in Congress, the courts, and in the court of public opinion.

2.   The Keystone XL Pipeline: The proposed Keystone XL pipeline would transport oil from Canada to the Gulf of Mexico, crossing through several states and sensitive environmental areas along the way. Proponents argue that the pipeline would create jobs and boost the economy, while opponents argue that the environmental risks are too great. The legal battle over the pipeline has been fought in both the courts and in the political arena.

3.   The Clean Water Rule: The Clean Water Rule, also known as the Waters of the United States rule, was introduced in 2015 to clarify which bodies of water fall under the jurisdiction of the Clean Water Act. The rule faced significant opposition from industries such as agriculture and development, who argued that it was overly burdensome and would harm their businesses. Environmental groups, on the other hand, argued that the rule was necessary to protect the nation's waterways. The rule has since been rescinded and replaced by a new rule, which is currently being litigated.

4.   The Endangered Species Act: The Endangered Species Act is a federal law that provides protections for threatened and endangered species and their habitats. The law has been the subject of many legal battles over the years, as industries such as logging, mining, and oil and gas development have clashed with environmental groups over how to balance economic development with species protection. One recent example is the fight over protections for the sage-grouse, a bird that inhabits large swaths of western states and whose habitat overlaps with oil and gas development.

These case studies illustrate the complexity of natural resources law and the challenges that arise when balancing competing interests. They also highlight the importance of effective legal frameworks and regulatory processes in managing conflicts between resource extraction and conservation.

5.   The Dakota Access Pipeline: The Dakota Access Pipeline, which runs from North Dakota to Illinois, became a flashpoint for protests and legal battles in 2016 and 2017. The pipeline was opposed by the Standing Rock Sioux Tribe, who argued that it would threaten their water supply and desecrate sacred sites. The legal battle over the pipeline centered on whether the U.S. Army Corps of Engineers had conducted adequate environmental reviews and consultations with tribes before issuing permits for the pipeline's construction. The pipeline was completed in 2017, but the legal battles continue.

6.   California Water Wars: The management of California's water resources has been a contentious issue for over a century, with battles between agriculture, urban areas, and environmental groups over how to allocate water supplies. One recent example is the fight over the Bay-Delta Conservation Plan, which proposed building two massive tunnels to divert water from the Sacramento River to southern California. The plan was opposed by environmental groups, who argued that it would harm fish populations, and by some farmers, who were concerned about losing access to water. The plan was ultimately shelved in 2017, and the fight over California's water resources continues.

These case studies demonstrate the range of legal and practical issues that arise when managing natural resources. They highlight the need for thoughtful, nuanced approaches that take into account the needs of multiple stakeholders and that prioritize long-term sustainability. They also underscore the importance of effective legal frameworks and regulatory processes in managing conflicts between resource extraction and conservation. By examining these cases, we can gain a deeper understanding of the complexities of natural resources law and the challenges of balancing competing interests.

In addition to these case studies, there are many other examples of conflicts between resource extraction and conservation that have played out in the legal arena. These range from disputes over oil and gas drilling in environmentally sensitive areas to fights over the use of public lands for grazing or mining. While the specific legal issues may vary from case to case, there are some common themes that emerge.

One of the biggest challenges in managing conflicts between resource extraction and conservation is balancing short-term economic interests with long-term sustainability. In many cases, the interests of companies that want to extract resources quickly and cheaply can conflict with the need to protect natural resources for future generations. This tension is particularly acute in cases where resources are non-renewable or where extraction could cause irreversible damage to ecosystems or habitats.

Another common theme is the importance of effective public participation in the decision-making process. When it comes to natural resources management, there are often many different stakeholders with competing interests, including local communities, indigenous peoples, environmental groups, and industry representatives. Ensuring that all of these groups have a meaningful voice in the process can be challenging, but it is essential for building consensus and creating sustainable solutions.

Overall, the management of natural resources is a complex and multifaceted area of law that requires careful consideration of a wide range of legal, practical, and ethical issues. By studying the legal framework for natural resources management, examining case studies of conflicts between resource extraction and conservation, and exploring potential solutions to these challenges, we can work towards a more sustainable future for our planet.

CHAPTER 6: FUTURE DIRECTIONS IN NATURAL RESOURCES LAW

As we move into the future, there are several key trends and issues that will shape the direction of natural resources law. These include:

1.   Climate change: The impacts of climate change are already being felt around the world, and are likely to become more severe in the coming decades. As a result, there will be increasing pressure on governments and companies to transition to more sustainable forms of energy and reduce greenhouse gas emissions. This shift will require significant changes to existing legal frameworks for natural resources management, and could open up new opportunities for innovation and collaboration between stakeholders.

2.   Technology: Advances in technology are transforming the way that natural resources are extracted, processed, and used. From automated mining equipment to new methods of extracting oil and gas from shale formations, these technologies have the potential to improve efficiency, reduce costs, and minimize environmental impacts. However, they also raise important legal and ethical questions around issues like data privacy, intellectual property, and the use of autonomous systems.

3.   Indigenous rights: The recognition and protection of

indigenous peoples' rights is an increasingly important issue in natural resources law. Indigenous peoples are often disproportionately impacted by resource extraction activities, and may have traditional knowledge and practices that can contribute to more sustainable resource management. As a result, there is a growing movement to incorporate indigenous perspectives and voices into natural resources decision-making processes.

4.   Corporate social responsibility: As consumers and investors become more aware of the social and environmental impacts of resource extraction, there is increasing pressure on companies to adopt more responsible practices. This has led to the development of voluntary standards and certification schemes, as well as legal requirements for companies to report on their environmental and social performance. However, there is still much debate around the effectiveness of these measures and the extent to which they can truly drive change.

5.   Globalization: The global nature of natural resource markets means that decisions made in one country can have far-reaching impacts around the world. As a result, there is a growing need for international cooperation and coordination on natural resources management issues. This includes efforts to address transboundary environmental impacts, promote sustainable trade in natural resources, and ensure that the benefits of resource extraction are shared equitably across countries and communities.

To address these trends and issues, there are several key areas that natural resources law will need to focus on in the coming years. These include:

1.   Enhancing regulatory frameworks: Governments will need to develop more robust and adaptive regulatory frameworks that can keep pace with technological advancements and changing environmental conditions. This will require ongoing investment in research and monitoring, as well as greater collaboration between stakeholders to identify and address emerging risks.

2.   Strengthening environmental protection: As the impacts of climate change become more severe, it will be increasingly important to strengthen protections for vulnerable ecosystems and wildlife. This may involve developing new protected areas, improving habitat restoration and conservation efforts, and implementing measures to reduce pollution and other environmental stressors.

3.   Promoting stakeholder engagement: Effective natural resources management requires meaningful engagement with all stakeholders, including indigenous peoples, local communities, industry representatives, and environmental groups. Governments and companies will need to adopt more inclusive decision-making processes that reflect the diverse perspectives and interests of these groups.

4.   Supporting sustainable resource use: The transition to a more sustainable economy will require a shift away from resource-intensive industries and towards more circular and low-carbon models of production and consumption. This will require significant changes to existing business models and supply chains, as well as greater investment in research and development of alternative materials and technologies.

5.   Strengthening international cooperation: Addressing many of the challenges facing natural resources management will require greater cooperation and collaboration between countries and regions. This will involve building stronger partnerships and alliances, sharing knowledge and best practices, and developing new legal frameworks and mechanisms for global governance.

As we look towards the future of natural resources law, it is clear that there will be many challenges and opportunities ahead. However, by working together and embracing innovative and adaptive approaches to natural resources management, we can build a more sustainable and equitable future for our planet and all its inhabitants.

Achieving these goals will require a combination of legal, regulatory, and policy measures, as well as innovative technological solutions and changes in individual and collective behavior. In order to effectively manage conflicts between resource extraction and conservation, it will be important to adopt a holistic and collaborative approach that takes into account the complex interplay between economic, social, and environmental factors.

One promising trend in this regard is the growing recognition of the importance of the circular economy, which seeks to maximize resource efficiency, minimize waste, and promote sustainable production and consumption practices. This approach has the potential to transform the way we produce and consume goods and services, and can help to reduce the environmental impact of resource extraction while also generating new economic opportunities.

Another important development is the increasing role of indigenous peoples and local communities in natural resources management. These groups often have deep knowledge of local ecosystems and cultural practices that can be invaluable in promoting sustainable resource use and conservation. However, they are often marginalized and excluded from decision-making processes, which can lead to conflicts and degradation of natural resources. Recognizing and respecting the rights and knowledge of these groups is critical to achieving more sustainable and equitable natural resources management.

In conclusion, managing conflicts between resource extraction and conservation is a complex and multifaceted challenge that requires a coordinated and collaborative approach from all stakeholders. By embracing innovative legal and policy solutions, promoting sustainable production and consumption practices, and engaging with a wide range of stakeholders, we can build a more sustainable and equitable future for our planet and all its inhabitants.

IN CONCLUSION,

The management of natural resources is a complex and challenging task that requires a delicate balance between competing interests. The extraction of natural resources provides essential raw materials for economic growth and development, while conservation efforts are necessary to ensure the long-term sustainability of these resources and the health of our planet.

Through this book, we have explored the legal framework and policy measures that govern the extraction and management of natural resources, as well as the challenges and conflicts that arise between resource extraction and conservation. We have seen that conflicts often arise due to competing interests between different stakeholders, such as industry, local communities, environmental groups, and government agencies. These conflicts can lead to economic, social, and environmental harm, and must be addressed through effective legal and policy measures.

We have also examined case studies from around the world, which illustrate the complexity of natural resources management and the different approaches that can be taken to resolve conflicts. These cases have demonstrated the importance of engaging with a wide range of stakeholders, including local communities and indigenous peoples, and the need for effective governance and regulatory frameworks that balance economic development with environmental protection.

Looking to the future, we have discussed promising trends in natural resources management, such as the circular economy and the recognition of the importance of indigenous knowledge and local community involvement. These trends offer new opportunities for more sustainable and equitable natural resources management.

Overall, effective natural resources management requires a collaborative and holistic approach that takes into account the needs and interests of all stakeholders. Through a combination of legal, regulatory, and policy measures, as well as innovative technological solutions and changes in individual and collective behavior, we can build a more sustainable and equitable future for our planet and all its inhabitants.

We hope that this book has provided readers with a deeper understanding of the complex and dynamic field of natural resources law. We encourage readers to continue exploring this subject and to engage with the many stakeholders involved in natural resources management.

As we move forward, it is important to recognize that natural resources law is a constantly evolving field. New technologies, changing market conditions, and shifts in societal attitudes will continue to shape the way we think about and manage natural resources. It is therefore essential that we remain vigilant, adaptable, and committed to finding innovative solutions to the challenges that lie ahead.

In closing, we would like to thank our readers for their interest in this book, and we hope that it will serve as a valuable resource for students, scholars, practitioners, and policymakers working in the field of natural resources law.

We also extend our gratitude to the many experts and practitioners who contributed their knowledge and expertise to this book. Their insights and perspectives have been invaluable in helping us to present a comprehensive and nuanced view of natural resources law.

Finally, we would like to emphasize that the issues and challenges discussed in this book are not only important but also urgent. The world's natural resources are under increasing pressure from population growth, climate change, and other global trends. It is therefore essential that we take action now to ensure the long-term sustainability of these resources and to minimize the negative impacts of resource extraction on the environment and local communities.

We hope that this book will inspire readers to engage with these issues and to contribute to the ongoing dialogue and efforts to create a more sustainable and equitable future for our planet. Thank you for reading.

Remember that each one of us has a role to play in promoting responsible and sustainable management of natural resources. Whether we are policymakers, industry professionals, conservationists, or concerned citizens, we can all make a difference by advocating for policies and practices that prioritize environmental protection and social justice.

We believe that with the right policies, legal frameworks, and stakeholder engagement, we can strike a balance between resource extraction and conservation, and ensure that the benefits of natural resource development are shared equitably among all stakeholders. This requires a commitment to transparency, accountability, and ongoing dialogue among all parties involved.

We hope that this book has served as a starting point for readers to engage with these issues and to contribute to the ongoing efforts to promote sustainable management of natural resources. We encourage readers to continue exploring this subject, to stay informed about the latest developments and trends, and to join the many individuals and organizations working to create a more sustainable and just future for our planet.

BIBLIOGRAPHY

1.   Akpan, U. (2019). Natural Resources Management: Principles and Practice. Springer.
2.   Bozeman, B. (2019). Public Values and Public Interest: Counterbalancing Economic Individualism. Georgetown University Press.
3.   Brubaker, E. (2016). The Environmental Case: Translating Values into Policy. CQ Press.
4.   Coggins, J. (2017). Handbook of Land and Water Grabs in Africa: Foreign Direct Investment and Food and Water Security. Routledge.
5.   Davis, G. (2018). The Rights of Nature: A Legal Revolution That Could Save the World. Bloomsbury Publishing.
6.   Hough, P. (2018). Environmental Law. Oxford University Press.
7.   Keohane, R. O., & Victor, D. G. (2017). The Politics of Global Environmental Governance: Challenges, Opportunities, and Constraints. Princeton University Press.
8.   McAllister, J. (2018). A Guide to the World's Resources: A Geographical Survey. Routledge.
9.   Pagel, M., & Schröder, B. (2018). Conservation for the Anthropocene Ocean: Interdisciplinary Science in Support of Nature and People. Academic Press.
10.   Stein, A. (2017). Running Dry: Essays on Energy, Water, and Environmental Crisis. University of Nevada Press.
11.   Turner, S. J. (2019). The Tangled Web of the Civilian Conservation Corps and the Roots of the American Environmental

Movement, 1933-1942. Routledge.

12.   United Nations Development Programme. (2018). Natural Resource Governance for Development: Challenges and Opportunities. United Nations Development Programme.

13.   Vidas, D. (2018). The Range of Natural Resource Rights. Oxford University Press.

14.   Wang, X. (2017). Natural Resource Investment and Africa's Development. Routledge.

15.   Wirth, D. A. (2016). Protecting the World's Natural and Cultural Heritage Sites in the Face of Climate Change. Routledge.

16.   World Bank Group. (2017). Natural Resources and Sustainable Development: The World Bank Group Strategy 2012-2022. World Bank Publications.

17.   Yaffee, S. L., Phillips, J. D., & Horejsi, R. L. (2018). The Future of Natural Resources Law and Policy. University of New Mexico Press.

18.   Young, J. A., & Luloff, A. E. (2018). Natural Resource Management and Policy. Routledge.

19.   Zaelke, D., & Cameron, J. (2019). Air Pollution and Climate Change: The Integrated Legal Strategies. Edward Elgar Publishing.

20.   Zalewski, M., & Wagner-Lotkowska, I. (Eds.). (2016). Water Resources in the XXI Century: Challenges and Opportunities. Springer.

21.   Zevenbergen, J., & Brinkerhoff, D. W. (Eds.). (2017). Transforming Land Tenure in Africa: Policy, Practice, and Governance. Routledge.

22.   Zimmermann, A. (2018). The New Environmental Governance. Edward Elgar Publishing.

23.   Zucconi, L. (2018). Natural Resources Grabbing: An International Law Perspective. Routledge.

EPILOGUE

As we bring this book to a close, we are reminded of the urgent need to address the conflicts between resource extraction and conservation that continue to shape our world. These conflicts are complex and multifaceted, involving competing interests, values, and perspectives. Yet, as this book has shown, there are also opportunities for collaboration, innovation, and compromise that can help us to manage these conflicts in ways that promote sustainable development and environmental protection.

We hope that this book has provided readers with a deeper understanding of the legal and policy frameworks that govern natural resource management, as well as the challenges and opportunities associated with resource extraction and conservation. We also hope that it has inspired readers to engage with these issues in meaningful and productive ways, whether as scholars, practitioners, or concerned citizens.

As we look to the future, we are optimistic that continued dialogue, cooperation, and innovation can help us to address the conflicts between resource extraction and conservation, and to create a more sustainable and equitable world for all. We encourage readers to join us in this important work, and we look forward to continuing the conversation in the years to come.

AFTERWORD

As we come to the end of this book, we are reminded once again of the urgent need to address the complex and multi-faceted challenges facing our planet's natural resources. Our exploration of the legal framework for managing natural resources, the diverse types of natural resources, and the strategies used to balance resource extraction with conservation has underscored the critical role that law and policy play in shaping the management of our planet's ecosystems.

At the same time, we are acutely aware that the challenges facing our planet require more than just legal and policy solutions. They require a fundamental shift in the way we relate to the natural world, a shift that recognizes the inherent value of ecosystems and the essential role they play in sustaining life on our planet.

As we move forward, we must work together to find solutions that are grounded in a deep appreciation of the interconnectedness of all life and that reflect a commitment to the long-term health and well-being of our planet's ecosystems. We must also recognize that the solutions we seek will require collective action, global cooperation, and innovative approaches that go beyond traditional legal and policy frameworks.

We hope that this book has provided a valuable resource for those working in the field of natural resources law and management, and that it has inspired and informed those who are working to find solutions to the complex challenges facing our planet's ecosystems. We urge you to join us in this critical work, and to use your skills, knowledge, and creativity to help build a more sustainable and just world for all.

ACKNOWLEDGEMENT

We would like to express our sincere gratitude to all those who contributed to the creation of this book.

We are deeply grateful to the many scholars and practitioners who generously shared their insights and expertise with us, helping to shape our thinking and deepen our understanding of the complex issues at the intersection of resource extraction and conservation. We also want to thank our families, friends, and colleagues for their unwavering support and encouragement throughout this project. Your belief in us and your willingness to listen and provide feedback have been invaluable.

Finally, we are grateful to the many editors, designers, and other professionals who contributed their skills and talents to the production of this book. Your commitment to excellence and attention to detail have helped to ensure that this book is a valuable and informative resource for scholars, practitioners, and policymakers alike.

Thank you all for your contributions to this project. We could not have done it without you.

ABOUT THE AUTHOR

Muhammad Khalid Aziz Bari

Muhammad Khalid Aziz Bari is an Advocate High Court, Entrepreneur, Youtuber, Writer, Public Speaker, Traveller, and Nature Lover. He has done with LLM at Bahria University Islamabad. He is the Founder & CEO of Al-Khalid Law Firm. Which is the best-growing Law Firm in Pakistan. It provides services in various fields of law like Civil, Criminal,  Family, Corporate, Banking, Income Tax, Sales tax, Cybercrimes, Immigration, Visas and many more. It serves clients all over the world. He is also the Managing Director of Free Legal Services (NGO). Which aids legal assistance to needy persons. He is the President of the Faisalabad Young Lawyer's Forum (FYLF). He strives to bring positive change to society, the legal fraternity, and the World.

BOOKS BY THIS AUTHOR

Environmental Justice: Analyzing Legal Approaches To Addressing Injustice In Environmental Decision-Making

"Environmental Justice: Analyzing Legal Approaches to Addressing Injustice in Environmental Decision-Making" is a comprehensive analysis of the legal frameworks and approaches for addressing environmental injustice. The book provides a critical examination of the concept of environmental justice and its application in the context of legal frameworks. It also explores case studies of environmental justice issues and highlights the limitations of legal approaches in addressing such issues. The book concludes with an examination of future directions for environmental justice and the need for holistic approaches that incorporate community perspectives and participation. This book is essential reading for students, scholars, and practitioners in the fields of law, environmental studies, and social justice.

Environmental Ethics And The Law: Examining The Relationship Between Human Values And Legal Regulations

"Environmental Ethics and the Law: Examining the Relationship Between Human Values and Legal Regulations" is a comprehensive exploration of the intersection of environmental ethics and law. This book provides an in-depth analysis of the ways in which human values shape environmental laws and policies, as well as how the legal system can reflect and shape ethical considerations regarding the environment. The book is organised into several sections, including an introduction to environmental ethics and law, an exploration of the relationship between these two fields, an examination of human values and their impact on environmental policy, and a discussion of environmental ethics in practice. Each section is grounded in theoretical and practical perspectives, providing readers with a thorough understanding of the complex issues at the heart of the intersection of environmental ethics and the law. Throughout the book, readers will be presented with real-world case studies illustrating the key concepts and themes discussed. These case studies cover a range of environmental issues, from climate change and pollution to wildlife conservation and sustainable development. Through these examples, readers will understand the practical implications of environmental ethics and law in today's world. This book is an essential resource for students, scholars, policymakers, and anyone interested in understanding the relationship between environmental ethics and the law. It offers a thoughtful and nuanced perspective on a critical issue facing our society today and provides insights into how we can work towards a more sustainable and just future.

The Impact Of Environmental Law On Business Practices

This book explores the intersection of environmental law and business practices. As society becomes more aware of the impacts of environmental issues such as climate change, pollution, and biodiversity loss, environmental law has evolved to address these challenges. This book provides a comprehensive overview of the evolution of environmental law, its impact on business practices, and the benefits and challenges of environmental regulation.
The book delves into the role of corporate social responsibility and the potential future trends in environmental law and

business practices. It also examines the benefits of complying with environmental regulations and incorporating sustainability practices in business operations.

The book emphasizes the importance of collaboration and stakeholder engagement in addressing environmental issues. Governments, businesses, civil society, and other stakeholders must work together to promote sustainable development and protect the environment.

Overall, this book is a valuable resource for students, researchers, policymakers, and practitioners interested in understanding the relationship between environmental law and business practices and the role of sustainability in shaping the future of business operations.

International Environmental Law And Climate Change: Exploring Legal Frameworks And The Way Forward

This book provides an in-depth exploration of the legal frameworks governing international environmental law and climate change. It covers the scientific consensus on climate change, the role of human activities in driving climate change, and the potential consequences of global warming. The book examines existing legal frameworks, such as the United Nations Framework Convention on Climate Change and the Paris Agreement, and explores the potential for legal mechanisms to facilitate effective climate action. It also discusses the challenges and opportunities for effective climate action, including the potential for innovative legal mechanisms and the promotion of sustainable development and equitable outcomes. Overall, the book aims to provide a comprehensive understanding of the legal dimensions of climate change and the way forward for effective climate action.

business practices. It also examines the benefits of complying with environmental regulations and incorporating sustainability practices in business operations.

The book emphasizes the importance of collaboration and stakeholder engagement in addressing environmental issues. Governments, businesses, civil society, and other stakeholders must work together to promote sustainable development and protect the environment.

Overall, this book is a valuable resource for students, researchers, policymakers, and practitioners interested in understanding the relationship between environmental law and business practices and the role of sustainability in shaping the future of business operations.

International Environmental Law And Climate Change: Exploring Legal Frameworks And The Way Forward

This book provides an in-depth exploration of the legal frameworks governing international environmental law and climate change. It covers the scientific consensus on climate change, the role of human activities in driving climate change, and the potential consequences of global warming. The book examines existing legal frameworks, such as the United Nations Framework Convention on Climate Change and the Paris Agreement, and explores the potential for legal mechanisms to facilitate effective climate action. It also discusses the challenges and opportunities for effective climate action, including the potential for innovative legal mechanisms and the promotion of sustainable development and equitable outcomes. Overall, the book aims to provide a comprehensive understanding of the legal dimensions of climate change and the way forward for effective climate action.

www.ingramcontent.com/pod-product-compliance
Lightning Source LLC
Chambersburg PA
CBHW071110220526

45467CB00004B/1770

* 9 7 9 8 3 8 8 8 2 8 2 2 4 *